BAT WING HALLOWEEN

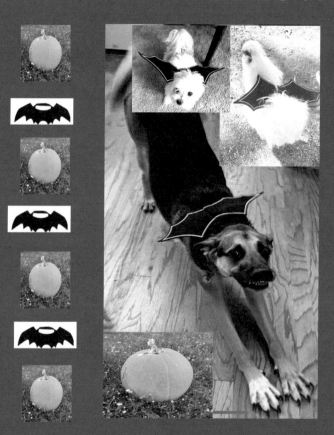

By

Susan Porter

BAT WING HALLOWEEN

WRITTEN BY SUSAN PORTER

PHOTOS BY SUSAN PORTER & TINA CARTER & KATELYNN FELTON

EDITED BY ALL MY FAVORITE MINIONS

TECHNICAL SUPPORT JAMES PORTER

Halloween is almost here. After learning how amazing bats are, we wanted to try on bat wings too! There were some party poopers, but the rest of us had a flapping good time!

Midnight

was, Scaredy Bat!

Mufausa

was too grumpy to wear bat wings.

 Our little Squirrel friend was just too squirrely to sit
still and try on bat wings.   He was batty enough
without them. He zoomed here, there, and
everywhere.

Snuggle flapped her beautiful wings,
but she did not look like a bat.

Ethel covered herself in mud, but she did not
look like a bat. She just looked like a dirty duck.

Oscar flapped his little wings while Lady Shadow cheered Him on, but it just wasn't the same as having bat wings.

Oscar tried on the bat wings, and they fit perfectly. He felt like he could fly and catch some bugs.

Oscar does like to eat bugs, but he has to eat the ones on the ground, because roosters can't fly.

Priscilla, **Wingnut**, & **Schultz**

were too busy practicing being flamingoes to try on bat wings.

Meanwhile, Polly C (C is for Chicken) was practicing her parrot impression.

Petri, Peepers, and Brunhilda were all *EGGceptionally* busy, so they didn't have time to try on bat wings.

 Lady Shadow didn't try on the bat wings, but she did look a little like a bat as a baby.

Our Colorado Cousins Pippa, Dudley, and Belle were too serious and slobbery to try on bat wings. Artie, however, was excited to try them on.

Artie thought he looked as amazing as a bat's squeak.

Pumpkin didn't want to wear bat wings because she was wearing her fancy orange bow.

Athena was wearing her Halloween pumpkin sweater, so she didn't try them on.

Our horse friend wasn't feeling very *neigh-borly,* so he didn't try on the batwings.

Oh Deer, this Colorado friend was too big for bat wings.

Bat wings aren't really her thing, but Cheeky loves any excuse to put on her Hula outfit.

The snake in the chicken coop was too slithery to try on bat wings.

The vultures on the roof were too spooky, and they had their own wings.

Rhino was way too busy kitten sitting his new baby sister, Queen Elizabeth, to try on bat wings.

He did do his vampire impression though.

Our little cousin, Peso the Degu, was too small to try on bat wings.

Oreo and Toga were in bat heaven at the idea of dressing up as that amazing night creature, the bat.

Toga felt like she was,

Super Bat!

Silly Oreo.

He can go from sweet, mild-mannered bat, to scary Vampire bat, faster than a bat can eat a mosquito. "*Hiss*" acting skills are very good.

  Apollo wasn't sure what face to make at first.

He decided to copy Oreo and make a vampire face.

"I vant to eat your candy."

 Jake also tried his vampire smile.

 All the vampire impressions frightened Magnolia.

Silly googly eyes helped her feel better.

They tried a few other costumes just for fun. Beaux decided to try a cat hat.

Athena thinks chameleons are cool. Oohh where'd she go? She's *chameleon-flaged.*

Oreo loves to eat! Who could be a better chef, than someone named after a cookie?

Our camel friends next door watched all the dress-up with interest, but they didn't think the bat wings, or other costumes, would fit over the humps on their backs.

We were so excited when we found a Little Brown Bat resting in the Umbrella outside. He didn't need to try on our bat wings. He had his very own. Happy Halloween little bat!

We had so much fun learning about bats and trying on bat wings, that we wanted to keep playing. So, we tried on some jolly hats.

Guess what Holiday is coming soon?

Bats are amazing! Here are a few things we learned about them, but there is so much more.

-Bats are not rodents or birds. They are flying mammals.

-Bats are nocturnal. That means they are awake at night, and sleep during the day.

-They don't have good eyesight; they use echolocation similar to whales and dolphins.

-Their grasp is strong enough to hold their own body weight upside down.

 -There are over 1,400 species of bats in the world.

-There are 40 species of bats in the United States.

 -The Little Brown Bat is the most common bat in the United States.

-The Common Vampire Bat can be found in Central and South America, and some Caribbean Islands.

-The smallest bat is the tiny Bumblebee Bat. It is an inch long.

-The largest bat is the Giant Golden-Crowned Flying Fox that has a wingspan of about 5 feet.

-Bats live in colonies anywhere from a few individuals up to a few hundred.

-A single bat can eat up to 600 insects per hour, and some can eat up to 1,500 insects a night.

-Some neighborhoods put up bat houses and are even using bats as natural pest control.

--Bats are very beneficial in getting rid of bugs.

Remember, even though they are cute, bats are wild animals. *Do Not* try to touch or hold them.